Windsor
SPLAT

LADDERBACK

Windsor
TRIPLE SPLAT

INDEX

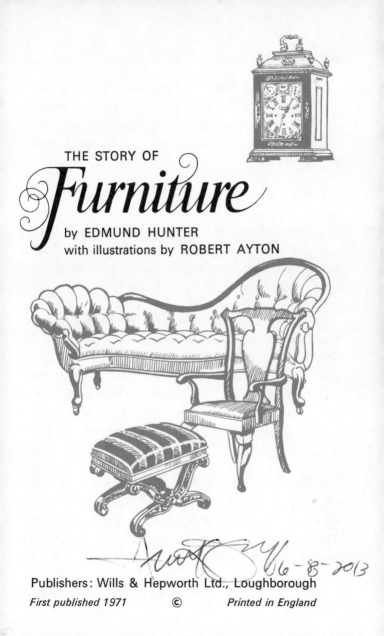

THE STORY OF

Furniture

by EDMUND HUNTER
with illustrations by ROBERT AYTON

Publishers: Wills & Hepworth Ltd., Loughborough

First published 1971   ©   *Printed in England*

Furniture of stone

The story of furniture follows very closely the story of houses and homes, of fashion – and of civilisation itself. The design, construction and use of furniture has changed throughout the ages with the changing pattern of people's lives.

To-day, most of us lead fairly settled lives. We normally stay in the same house or flat for several years at a time and furnish it comfortably. Many homes are fitted with every kind of labour-saving device and often with central heating as well. A wide range of furniture is available at prices most people can afford.

This was not so in days gone by. The earliest furniture was made of stone. We know of this because of discoveries in such prehistoric dwellings as those at Skara Brae in the Orkney islands. It consisted of crude stone tables and benches. There were no beds as we know them, but stone platforms probably covered with bracken and animal skins. This is how people probably lived 4,000 years ago.

Before the Normans came to Britain there was still very little furniture in existence. Ordinary people's lives were too insecure for them to have many possessions and they were often only too glad to have four walls and a roof as protection from the weather.

0 7214 0287 9

The interior of a hut 4,000 years ago

Stages of furniture development

Since those far-off days, wood has been the most important material for furniture making. The Ancient Egyptians used it in the furnishing of their great tombs and palaces. When the Romans extended their empire into western Europe, they found vast forests of oak which provided plenty of timber for the building of their ships and for the furniture used in the houses of the wealthy.

However, this book tells the story of furniture from the time of the Normans until the present day. There seem to have been roughly four main stages of furniture development.

The first stage was from the Norman conquest through the Middle Ages and up to the time of Cromwell; a rough and ready age full of trouble and strife and very little comfort. Then from the reign of Charles I to the time of Queen Victoria came a stage of great advancement when furniture of high quality was designed and made for special purposes. People spent more time indoors and this had an influence on the furnishing of their homes. Another big change came about during the reign of Queen Victoria and up to the First World War. And finally we come to the furniture of our modern age.

During the first two stages particularly, nearly all the furniture belonged to the nobility and other wealthy people. The remainder of the population enjoyed little comfort.

A Norman saw-pit. Sawing planks from a log

The Great Hall

During the Middle Ages (also known as the medieval period – from about 1066 until about 1485) the nobility lived in castles and manor houses. A large part of their lives was spent outdoors hunting and fighting, and because of this the internal arrangement of their homes was of the barest kind. The Great Hall was the eating, living and sleeping room. At one end there was often a low platform for the use of the nobleman, his family and important guests, while the main area of the hall was occupied by retainers and servants.

The platform was furnished with a wooden table and benches and probably a more elaborate, carved chair for the head of the household. Loose cushions might be provided for the greater comfort of the people sitting on these hard seats, and for added warmth and colour, tapestries were often hung on the wall behind the platform.

In the main part of the hall lived the retainers and servants who sat on backless benches at trestle tables. There were also one or two chests in which were stored the master's table-linen, drinking goblets and valuables. These chests could also be used as seats. The hall was sometimes used as a courtroom and assembly area. At the command, 'A-hall, a-hall' the trestle tables were quickly cleared away, leaving the whole area free of obstructions.

Portable furniture

The furniture of medieval times was made so that it could be taken to pieces and put together again quickly. Table tops and trestles were easily dealt with but even the less movable items were often made portable. The various sections of a piece of furniture were jointed together and secured in position by long oak pins. When the furniture had to be dismantled the pins were driven out and the sections simply taken apart.

This portability was important. Most of the barons of the time had several estates in different parts of the country. Furniture was expensive and difficult to obtain and few could afford to have more than one 'fully-furnished' castle. It was therefore necessary to carry the one set around during visits to other estates. This method also prevented the baron's enemies from removing all his belongings whilst he was away on other business; a very likely possibility!

The heaviest pieces of furniture were the chests, which were more solidly made. Furniture, tapestries, ornaments, valuables and weapons were all taken along when the baron, his family and his retainers travelled around the country.

Removing the portable furniture to another castle

The solar

Toward the end of the medieval period, other smaller rooms were added to the castles and manor houses. The most important of these was known as the *solar*. This was what might be called a 'retiring room' where the nobleman and his family could gain a little privacy away from all the people in the main hall.

The chief piece of furniture in the solar was the bed. In medieval times this consisted of a simple wooden frame, usually fitted with a canopy above and draped around with curtains. The curtains could be drawn back during the daytime when the bed was used as a couch. The remaining items of furniture often included a chest for storing clothes, a simple cupboard, a small table and possibly a stool. A plaited rush mat might cover the floor and curtains could be hung at the window. The furniture was rather plain and lightly made because, we must remember, it still might all have to be packed up and moved to another estate at short notice.

Later, in Tudor times, when life became more settled the solar furniture was made more elaborately, nearly always of oak and beautifully carved. The four-poster beds of Tudor times became a great feature and some examples are still in existence.

The parlour

By the time Henry VIII came to the throne of England in 1509, the country had become more prosperous, social conditions had improved and rich merchants as well as the nobility were looking for better living conditions.

The Great Hall, which might still be used for banquets and other special occasions, had lost much of its importance. A gallery was built around it to form a landing, giving access to rooms on an upper floor. Other rooms were added, including a study and summer and winter *parlours*, the last named eventually becoming the dining room.

Oak panelling had come into fashion and the walls of the parlour and parts of the furniture were often covered with panels carved in a pattern known as *linenfold*. There was a table at which meals were eaten and benches for people to sit on. There might be one richly-carved oak chair for the master of the house. An early form of sideboard, called a *buffet*, was also included as a serving table, and cupboards built into it were used for storing the eating and drinking utensils. The floor was often covered with loose rushes or rush matting.

It can be seen that, in spite of improvements, early Tudor furnishing was still not really comfortable.

Elizabethan furniture

Living conditions, at least near the large towns, continued to improve so that skilled tradesmen and yeoman farmers joined the merchants and noblemen in seeking better houses and greater comfort. England during the reign of Elizabeth I (1558 – 1603) became rich and powerful.

Life was more secure, so houses no longer had to be fortified against attack and it was no longer necessary to carry everything away during trips to other parts of the country. Furniture could now be properly 'joined'. Wealthy houses had oak-panelled walls – a more simple panelling now, not the complicated linenfold of earlier times. Heavily-decorated plaster ceilings became popular and ornamental fireplaces became the focal point of living rooms.

A beautifully-carved four-poster bed featured in several rooms, not just in one, and solid, well-made tables with carved legs were used for the main meals. In Elizabethan homes the bed and the table were among owners' most prized possessions.

Properly-jointed, four-legged stools took the place of the earlier rough benches, and chairs became popular. These sometimes had gaily-coloured cushions and covers to make them more attractive and comfortable. A *press*, or wall cupboard, was used for hanging up clothes in bedrooms. This was the forerunner of our modern wardrobe.

A four-poster bed and other Elizabethan furniture

Furniture of the farmhouse and cottage

So far our story has been chiefly concerned with the homes and furniture of the wealthy but, of course, the mass of the population lived in much more humble circumstances. Until about 1650, the time of Oliver Cromwell and the Civil War in England, all the furniture was hand-made and hand-carved. It was difficult to obtain and very expensive.

Labourers in country and town had to do the best they could to furnish their farmhouses and cottages. For many centuries they had very few possessions and what they had was rough, bare and of the simplest form. Local woods were used which were not as strong or as long-lasting as the fine oaks from which the furniture of the wealthy was made. Nevertheless, cottage furniture improved during the years and by the beginning of the seventeenth century it was sturdily made and had a simple character of its own.

By the end of the century (1700), farmers and middle-class people all over the country were building pleasant homes for themselves and furnishing them with items not as ornate as those in the great houses of the rich, but of a good standard of quality.

The furniture of the farmhouse and middle-class home soon after the year 1700

Veneers and decoration

Some time about 1660, furniture-makers began to decorate their handiwork, adding woods of different kinds to the basic oak piece. The earliest form of this art was known as *chip-work* in which recesses were carved in the solid oak and pieces of another wood *inlaid* to form a pattern.

The next type of decoration to be used was *parquetry*, in which rectangular pieces of wood of different colours were placed together to form a pattern and glued down to a base. This process in one form is still used to-day for parquet floors.

Finally came *marquetry* which was the most difficult and expensive form of furniture decoration. In this process, thin slices of wood about one-sixteenth of an inch thick were used. These were known as *veneers*. They were shaped to make up intricate designs, often of flowers, and glued onto the basic furniture material.

Marquetry was first developed in Holland around 1625 and later carried on in England and France as well. Good, marqueteered, antique furniture is in great demand to-day by collectors and it usually fetches very high prices. Much of it can still be seen in our 'stately homes'.

A walnut cabinet decorated with panels of marquetry (about 1680)

Furniture for special purposes

After the Great Fire of London in 1666 came a new age in furniture making, an age in which tremendous changes took place and many advances were made. The large, heavy pieces of furniture made by the carpenters and joiners of earlier times no longer suited people's living habits. Lighter, more movable pieces were in demand. The cabinet-maker took over the task of designing and making furniture for special purposes.

A machine, the lathe, came into use and with it a 'turner' was able to produce large quantities of legs of various shapes for tables, chairs, sideboards and cupboards, and also chair arms and backs.

Charles II was responsible for much of the improvement in the standard of comfort and design of the time. He had been greatly influenced by the fashions he saw while in exile on the continent, particularly in France. On his return to the throne he encouraged standards of design that were later copied all over the country. Among the new kinds of furniture he introduced were bookcases, writing desks, cabinets, small side-tables and dressing tables. The new, faster methods of manufacture enabled more people to enjoy these new comforts.

About this time lacquered furniture also became popular. This was furniture decorated in coloured varnishes – an art which originated in the East. A lacquered cabinet is shown in the illustration opposite.

Chairs for everyone

The years just before 1700 also saw two other changes: a change from oak to walnut as the chief material from which good furniture was made, and a great improvement in the design and availability of chairs.

At about that time chair-making became a craft on its own and was separated from the job of cabinet-making. Until then chairs were used very little and even the best of them had hard seats and upright backs. Now, chair designers began to bear in mind the shape of the human body. Seats became upholstered and soft to sit on, while the backs were sometimes given a slight curve. The day-bed (a chair with a long seat) made its appearance.

The invention of the lathe had made it possible to produce chairs more cheaply and in greater quantity so that people living in smaller houses and cottages could also afford them. Many different styles were produced, such as the *ladderback*, *wheelback*, *stickback* and *Windsor*.

These simple chairs were made out of a variety of materials, often by local craftsmen, but chairs and other furniture for the fine mansions of the period were often made in walnut, a wood with a beautiful grain which could be highly polished.

London and High Wycombe became the chief furniture-making centres of Britain.

Top: A day-bed
Below: The variety of chairs available
for the rich after 1700

24

More about chairs

The early development of chairs has already been dealt with, and we have shown that they gradually ceased to be just things to sit on (often uncomfortably) and became more decorative.

Chair legs became more shapely, and various designs of chairs to seat two or three people side by side (settees) made their appearance – and also couches and sofas. In the illustration opposite are shown some of the variations produced in the seventeenth and eighteenth centuries.

Armchairs and settees were often fitted with *wings* to keep cold draughts away from the occupant's face. Some modern armchairs still copy this feature from the old designs – even though in the modern, centrally heated home there are no cold draughts!

Comfort became an essential part of every chair design, and more and more were upholstered – using horse-hair stuffing. This process went on into the Victorian period. Notice the buttoned upholstery of the Victorian sofa shown opposite.

Upholstered chairs and settees

1680

1610

1680

1720

1730

1850

Furniture with cupboards and drawers

Earlier in this book we have seen how medieval homes were almost devoid of all furniture except tables and benches for eating, a bed for the owners to sleep in, chests for storage purposes and perhaps a set of shelves to hold eating and drinking utensils and to display gold and silver ornaments. A 'cupboard' was actually a board upon which cups were set!

Closed cupboards were first used in the 'fifteenth century and were known as *livery cupboards*. They held the livery, that is, food and drink and possibly spare candles. Surprisingly enough they were originally put into bedrooms, possibly to protect the contents from thieves. The doors were pierced with tracery for ventilation. Livery cupboards were later moved into the room used for dining and were replaced in the reign of Charles II by *buffets* which could also be used as serving tables. These eventually became the sideboards of to-day.

Chests of drawers were introduced in the seventeenth century. Later they were made very high and known as *tallboys*. With the development of printing, books became more widely read and glass-fronted bookcases were produced. These have altered little over the years except in materials and methods of decoration.

At about the same time, the writing desk, or *bureau*, made its appearance. It had a sloping top which opened out to form a flat surface. Inside were shelves and pigeon-holes to take the writing materials. Some modern bureaux still adopt the same principle.

A Court Cupboard 1600

An early standing cupboard 1500

Queen Anne Tallboy 1710

A bureau cabinet 1725

An age of elegance

Soon after 1700 large quantities of mahogany were being imported from the West Indies and were used to make some of the finest furniture.

As usual, the new fashions started with the nobility and wealthy, and nearly always from London. But by now, the middle-classes had acquired a taste for more refined living and they too collected around them many elegant pieces of furniture. They travelled abroad, trading with other countries, and brought new ideas into London on their return. The developing skill of the architect became available to more people, and whole rooms were designed to the last detail. The work of individual furniture designers and cabinet-makers was much sought after, and you will read about some of these men in the next chapter.

Veneers of mahogany, rosewood, satinwood and other rare timbers were cleverly used in marquetry to make the furniture as decorative as possible. One might be tempted to think that, with all this finery, houses during this period were just showplaces, but this would be wrong. People spent a great deal of time indoors and that is why they made their homes bright and comfortable.

The elegant surroundings of the wealthy in the Georgian period after 1714

Great names

The eighteenth century was a period of superb furniture making, and the names of four men stand out above all others as masters of their craft. Because they are so important, everyone interested in furniture and furnishing should know something about them.

Thomas Chippendale, who died in 1779, was the first and perhaps the most famous of the four. He was a furniture designer who published a book on the subject. His styles were copied by many cabinet-makers in London and elsewhere in Britain as well as in overseas countries.

George Hepplewhite lived during the same period as Chippendale and was a cabinet-maker. His name is mostly associated with a style of furniture which immediately followed the Chippendale period.

Thomas Sheraton, last of the great English designers and who died in 1806, is chiefly known by his published books on furniture design which helped to create a style or trend. He was purely a designer and as far as is known did not actually make any furniture himself.

Robert Adam, although he carried out some designing of individual pieces of furniture at about the same time, is more famous as an architect and designer of complete interiors. Adam fireplaces are particularly well-known products of his skill and many fine examples can be seen to-day.

The products of four great furniture designers

● Chippendale
● Hepplewhite
● Sheraton
● Adam

The Regency period

The Regency period covered about twenty-five years during the early part of the nineteenth century – from 1811 to 1835. It takes its name from the Prince Regent of the time (later to become George IV). This was a time when towns like Brighton, Bath, Cheltenham and Leamington Spa became famous as fashionable health resorts. It was the time of the dandy, Beau Brummell and of John Nash, the architect who designed the Royal Pavilion at Brighton which still contains some of its original furnishing.

Regency terraced houses are famous. In contrast to the elaborately-decorated rooms of the eighteenth century, their interiors were more restrained and provided a suitable background for gaily-coloured furniture. This was often made of dark rosewood with inlays of brass, or of beechwood painted in black and gold. Sofas and footstools upholstered in bright, striped silk, and cane-bottomed chairs, provided the main seating accommodation. Other items of furniture were also lightly made and brightly decorated. Gilt mirrors, draped, gold-fringed curtains and plain wallpaper were a feature of this period.

Regency furniture

Tables for dining and other purposes

We have read that in medieval times many people ate at one table, so it had to be a very long one. Because the table also had to be portable, the top usually rested on removable supports, called trestles. When people's lives grew more settled – as in Elizabethan times – the need for portability became less important, dining tables were given permanent legs which were nearly always carved by hand. A later development was the table with a draw-leaf at each end which could be pulled out to make the table longer for large parties. This draw-leaf arrangement still has its uses in modern homes. Tables used by the wealthy usually had carving or inlay work along the sides as well as carving round the legs.

The gate-leg table, with side legs that could be swung outward to support two hinged flaps, was often used for meals after about 1630.

In the eighteenth and nineteenth centuries came tables which were used for purposes other than dining, as writing tops, as somewhere to stand flower arrangements or on which to play cards. These were primarily of walnut or rosewood and later of mahogany, often beautifully decorated by carving or marquetry and sometimes with marble surfaces. They were of many different shapes and sizes. The *dumb waiter* was an interesting example. It consisted of a series of circular tables one above the other, from which people could help themselves to the various eatables placed on them.

Elizabethan 1570

Jacobean
1630

Georgian
1730

Georgian
1795

Georgian
1765

Regency 1815

The beginnings of the machine age

During the second half of the eighteenth century the Industrial Revolution came to Britain and with it a social change took place all over the country. Until then England had been a land of 'gentlemen', merchants, craftsmen, farmers and traders. The coming of the steam engine and other machinery brought people into the towns where they could earn money in the factories that were springing up everywhere.

For a good many years furniture escaped the effects of this new machine age, and until the end of the Regency period continued to be largely hand-made to first-class designs. But toward the end of the Regency period a change began to take place. People began to judge each other's success by the size of their houses and the amount of furniture they possessed. Quality tended to give way to quantity, and manufacturers grew more concerned with how much money they could make rather than with the quality of the goods they produced.

The great change was not all bad, however. Machine-made furniture was generally cheaper, and this meant that more and more people could enjoy more comfort. Some craftsmen still produced fine furniture which could be bought by those who could afford it.

Machine-made furniture becomes available to the less wealthy

Furniture during the reign of Queen Victoria

During the long reign of Queen Victoria (1837 – 1901), changes in furniture design continued. The light, gaily-decorated pieces of the Georgian and Regency periods gradually became less fashionable; rooms became more cluttered and the elegance disappeared. This was a period of solid prosperity in England – though mainly for the upper and middle classes. Many people spent their whole lives in one house and, as likely as not, died in the same house in which they had been born.

Furniture, as usual, reflected the way of living. Victorian furniture was solid, comfortable stuff, usually made of mahogany and constructed to last a lifetime. The middle-class Victorian home usually had a very overcrowded appearance. Walls were covered in heavily patterned paper and hung with pictures of all kinds; there were ornaments on the mantlepiece, on every conceivable shelf and ledge, and there was always at least one aspidistra plant in the 'parlour'.

Chairs and couches of various shapes and sizes were often padded with black horsehair and covered in velvet, their backs protected from greasy heads by *antimacassars*. Gas was sometimes used for lighting, the burners being suspended either from a central *gaselier* or from brackets on the walls.

A Victorian room

Furniture for entertainment

From Anglo-Saxon times right up to the twentieth century, people made their own entertainment wherever they gathered and often in their own homes. This is something we no longer have to do because the radio, television, cinema and record player provide us with ready-made entertainment. However, it would be sad if there were not people who still preferred to make their own entertainment – or at least a part of it, and one must hope that there will be more and more who come to know the pleasure of making their own music.

Keyboard musical instruments are also pieces of furniture, and they first became popular during the sixteenth century. The clavichord and virginal (Queen Elizabeth I played a virginal) were not provided with special legs but were stood on a table. The spinet which followed was complete with support and legs.

At the beginning of the eighteenth century came the harpsichord which was a more powerful type of spinet and bore a close family resemblance to the grand piano which was to follow.

The first piano was made in Germany and introduced into Britain toward the end of the eighteenth century. In the Victorian period the grand piano became a familiar piece of furniture in most large homes, and the less bulky, upright instrument was popular in smaller houses.

42   Musical instruments as furniture

Virginal on a table

Harpsichord

Upright Grand Piano

Modern times

The fourth and latest stage of furniture development began after the First World War (1914 – 1918) and the trends begun at that time have been continuing ever since. Motor cars came into increasing use, allowing families to get out and about more, and the cinema drew people out of their homes in the evenings. Houses built after that war became more compact and easier to run. In complete contrast to the Victorian period, furniture was made lighter, this being possible because of new materials. By the 1930's a certain number of tubular steel pieces, especially chairs, came into fashion.

Following the Second World War (1939 – 1945) when domestic servants were almost impossible to obtain and housewives went out to work in offices and factories, labour-saving ideas rapidly increased both in the design of homes as well as in their furnishings. To-day, veneers are used, not for elaborate decoration as in the past, but to give a fine, polished finish to inexpensive basic materials. Steel and plastics of all kinds are also playing an increasing part in the making of carefully designed items of furniture enabling them to be light, movable, colourful and comfortable.

Of course, some people still collect the old, hand-made furniture, and some 'reproduction' or imitation antique furniture is made for those who prefer it.

Bedroom furniture

Up to about 1750, the great four-poster bed with its carved head panel and supports was in fashion. By 1800, however, beds had become much lighter and in Victorian times they were generally mass-produced in iron or brass and with a wire mesh or spring base on which was placed a feather mattress. Wooden beds became popular again after the First World War when lighter, more modern designs were introduced.

Mirrors came into general use between the years 1600 and 1700. Later they became part of 'dressing-tables' which consisted of a base containing drawers for toilet preparations and a mirror (or mirrors) which could be swivelled.

Wash-stands were included in bedrooms between 1700 and 1900. On these stood a jug of water and a basin into which water could be poured for washing. It was only when bathrooms were included in the majority of houses, and tap water from mains became generally available, that the wash-stand was no longer a necessary piece of furniture.

To-day the trend is to 'build-in' the wardrobes, chests of drawers and dressing tables into the structure of the room and not have them as separate pieces of furniture. This saves space and allows more room for movement.

An Elizabethan and a modern bedroom

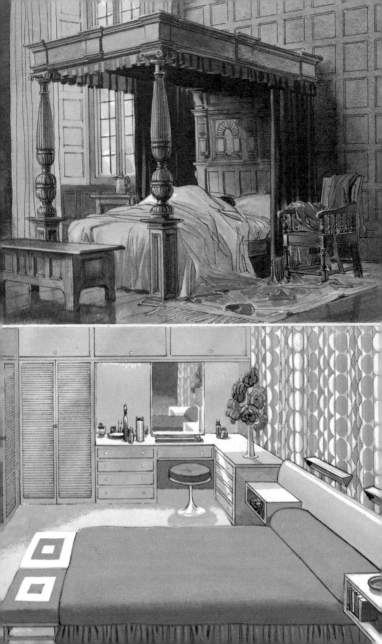

Table-ware

In Norman times table-ware consisted of wooden or metal *chargers* (A) into which were put the main portions of food. Diners eating at the table took their helpings from the chargers, cutting them up with their own dagger-like knives. They ate the meal with their fingers, using a piece of bread as a plate. Later, wooden or horn spoons came into use. It was not until after 1600 that forks made their appearance. Drinking was originally done from horns (B) and later from cups and goblets, filled from metal jugs (C).

Before and during Elizabethan times very rich people ate from gold and silver plates and drinking vessels. Those less rich used plates and mugs (D) made from pewter (an alloy of tin with other metals). Pottery became more fashionable later in the seventeenth century. Developments in the manufacture of glass made this material more popular, particularly for wine decanters and glasses (E and F).

Silver continued to be used into the eighteenth century for the finest dinner, tea and coffee services, but a new silver-like material called Sheffield Plate (G), which was cheaper, was often used instead. Porcelain crockery (H) from Staffordshire and Derby also became very popular. By this time there was a wide variety of dishes for meats, vegetables, soups and sauces, often made in very elaborate shapes.

'A' 1100

'B' 1400

'C' 1400

'D' 1610

'E' 1600

'F' 1700

1730

1750

1780

'H' 1800

'G' 1805

'G' 1850

Clocks and lights

The first sixteenth century clocks (A) had only one hand and were operated by weights suspended on chains. The clocks were usually fixed to the wall so that the weights could hang down freely. A swinging pendulum and an extra hand were added during the seventeenth century and some clocks were also made with coil-spring operation (B). The pendulum types were enclosed in long cases to give them more protection and they were known as long case, or *grandfather* clocks (C). The cases were often decorated to match the particular style of furniture in fashion. Coil-spring clocks were enclosed in a variety of decorative cases (D) and eventually found a permanent position on almost every mantlepiece – where they are usually located to-day.

Lighting in medieval times was by candles or torches (E) held by spikes fixed to the walls. Later a central fitting or *candlebeam* was introduced which held four candles. By Elizabethan times, simple *chandeliers* were being used and these gradually developed until, in the eighteenth century, they became beautiful, elaborately-decorated affairs, often incorporating a mass of cut-glass pendants (F). Candlesticks (G and H) – silver for the rich – were used for tables.

Oil lamps (I) provided the chief source of lighting for the Victorians until the introduction of gas (J). Electric lighting was first introduced at the end of the nineteenth century.

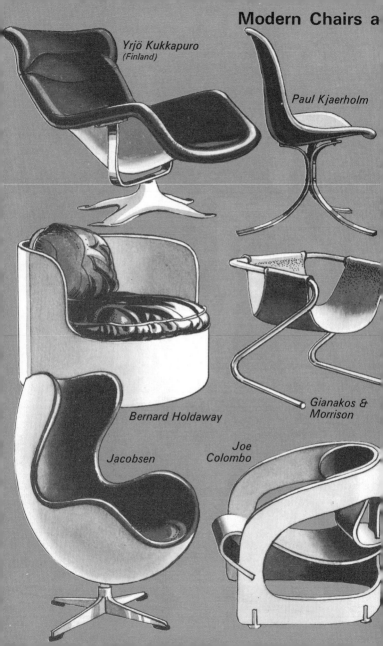

Yrjö Kukkapuro
(Finland)

Paul Kjaerholm

Bernard Holdaway

*Gianakos &
Morrison*

Jacobsen

*Joe
Colombo*